SPANISH FOR BEGIN...

Angela Wilkes

Illustrated by John Shackell

Designed by Roger Priddy
Edited by Nicole Irving
Language Consultant: Manuela Gomez

CONTENTS

About this book

Going abroad is much more fun if you can speak a little of the language. This book shows you that learning another language is a lot easier than you might think. It teaches you the Spanish you will find useful in everyday situations.

You can find out how to . . .

talk about yourself,

and your home,

count and tell the time,

say what you like,

find your way around

and ask for what you want in shops.

How you learn

Picture strips like this show you what to say in each situation. Read the speech bubbles and see how much you can understand by yourself, then look up any words you do not know. Words and phrases are repeated again and again, to help you remember them.

The book starts with really easy things to say and gets more difficult towards the end.

New words

All the new words you come across are listed on each double page, so you can look them up as you go along. If you forget any words you can look them up in the glossary on pages 46-48. *If you see an asterisk by a word, it means that there is a note about it at the bottom of the page.

Grammar

Boxes like this around words show where new grammar is explained. You will find Spanish easier if you learn some of its grammar, or rules, but don't worry if you don't understand it all straightaway. You can look up any of the grammar used in the book on pages 42-43.

Internet links*

If you have access to a computer with an Internet connection, you can try out the Web sites described at the top of each double page. For links to these sites go to **www.usborne-quicklinks.com**

Puzzles

Throughout the book there are puzzles and quizzes (with answers on pages 44-45). You'll find more puzzles that you can download for free at the Usborne Quicklinks Web site: **www.usborne-quicklinks.com**

Practising your Spanish

Write all the new words you learn in a notebook and try to learn a few every day. Keep going over them and you will soon remember them.

Ask a friend to keep testing you on your Spanish. Even better, ask someone to learn Spanish with you so that you can practise on each other.

Quiero...

Try to get to Spain for your holidays, and speak as much Spanish as you can. Don't be afraid of making mistakes. No one will mind.

* For more information on using the Internet, see inside the front cover.

Saying "Hello and Goodbye"

The first thing you should know how to say in Spanish is "Hello". There are different greetings for different times of day. Here you can find out what to say when.

In Spain it is polite to add **señor**, **señora** or **señorita** when you greet people you don't know. You say **señor** to men, **señora** to women and **señorita** to girls.

Saying "Hello"

This is how to say "Hello" to your friends.

This is more polite and means "Have a good day".

This is how you say "Good evening" to someone.

Saying "Goodbye"

Adiós means "Goodbye".

These are different ways of saying "See you again".

Saying "Goodnight"

You say "Buenas noches" in the evening and at bedtime.

How are you?

This is how to greet someone and ask how they are.

This person is saying that she is fine, thank you . . .

. . . but this one is saying things aren't too good.

¿Cómo estás?

This list shows you the different ways of saying how you are, from very well to terrible. What do you think each of the people here would say if you asked them how they were?

muy bien	very well
bien	well
bastante bien	quite well
no muy bien	not very well
muy mal	terrible

What is your name?

Here you can find out how to ask someone their name and tell them yours, and how to introduce your friends. Read the picture strip and see how much you can understand. Then try doing the puzzles on the page opposite.

New words

yo	I
tú	you
él	he
ella	she
ellos	they (male)
ellas	they (female)
¿cómo te llamas?	what are you called?
¿cómo se llama él/ella?	what is he /she called?
¿cómo se llaman ellos/ellas?	what are they called?
yo me llamo	I am called
él se llama	he is called
ella se llama	she is called
ellos/ellas se llaman	they are called
¿quién es?	who is that?
es	that is
mi amigo	my friend (male)
mi amiga	my friend (female)
¿y tú?	and you?
sí	yes
no	no

Ellos and ellas

There are two words for "they" in Spanish: **ellos** and **ellas**. When you are talking about boys or men, you say **ellos** and when you are talking about girls or women, you say **ellas**.

If you are talking about boys and girls or men and women together, you say **ellos**.

Buenos días, ¿cómo te llamas?

Mario, ¿y tú?

Yo me llamo Alicia.

Introducing friends

Es mi amigo. Se llama Pedro.

¿Quién es?

Es mi amiga. Se llama María.

¿Cómo se llaman?

Se llaman Pablo y Juan.

6

What are they called?

Can you answer these questions in Spanish?

¿Cómo se llama mi amiga?

¿Cómo te llamas?

¿Cómo se llama?

¿Cómo se llaman?

Who is who?

Can you answer the questions below the picture?

Hola, ¿cómo estás?

Bien, gracias.

Adiós, Nicolás.

¿Es Ana?

Sí, es Ana.

Adiós.

Es Juan.

¿Quién es?

No, yo me llamo Miguel.

¿Te llamas Mario?

¿Cómo te llamas?

Amalia, ¿y tú?

Who is talking to Juan?
Who is talking to Amalia?

Who is called Miguel?
Who is talking to him?

Who is called Ana?
Who is going home?

Can you remember?

How would you ask someone their name?
How would you tell them your name?

You have a friend called Amalia. How would you introduce her to someone?
How would you tell someone your friend is called Daniel?

Finding out what things are called

Everything on this picture has its name on it. See if you can learn the names for everything, then try the memory test at the bottom of the opposite page. You can find out what **el** and **la** mean at the bottom of the page.

la chimenea

el tejado

el Sol

el pájaro

¡ Buenos días!

el nido

el árbol

la ventana

la flor

la casa

la puerta

Esta es mi casa.

el garaje

la verja

el gato

el perro

el coche

El and la words*

All Spanish nouns are either masculine or feminine. The word you use for "the" shows what gender the noun is. The word for "the" is **el** before masculine (m) nouns and **la** before feminine (f) ones. It is best to learn which word to use with each noun. "A" or "an" is **un** before **el** words and **una** before **la** words.

el Sol	sun	**el nido**	nest	**la ventana**	window
el árbol	tree	**el pájaro**	bird	**la puerta**	door
el tejado	roof	**el garaje**	garage	**la flor**	flower
el gato	cat	**el coche**	car	**la casa**	house
el perro	dog	**la chimenea**	chimney	**la verja**	fence

*The word for "the" is **el**, and not the same as the word for "he", **él**, which has a stress mark. You can read more about stress marks on page 41.

Asking what things are called

Don't worry if you don't know what something is called in Spanish. To find out what it is just ask someone **¿qué es esto?** Look at the list of useful phrases below, then read the picture strip to see how to use them.

¿qué es esto?	what is that?
es . . .	that is . . .
también	also
en español	in Spanish
en inglés	in English

¿Qué es esto?

Es una flor.

¿Es esto también una flor?

No, es un árbol.

¿Qué es esto en español?

Es una puerta.

¿Y esto qué es?

Es un perro.

¿Qué es esto en inglés?

A dog!

Can you remember?

Cover up the opposite page and see if you can name all of these things in Spanish. Don't forget to say whether they are **el** or **la** words.

9

Where do you come from?

Here you can find out how to ask people where they come from. You can also find out how to ask if they speak Spanish.

New words

¿de dónde eres?	where do you come from?
soy de	I come from
¿dónde vives?	where do you live?
vivo en . . .	I live in . . .
¿hablas . . ?	do you speak . . ?
hablo . . .	I speak . . .
un poco	a little
español	Spanish
inglés	English
alemán	German
este/esta es	this is (m/f)
nosotros/as	we (m/f)
vosotros/as	you (plural, m/f)
ustedes	you (polite)

Countries

Alemania	Germany
Inglaterra	England
Francia	France
la India*	India
Escocia	Scotland
Austria	Austria
España	Spain
Hungría	Hungary

Where do you come from?

Do you speak Spanish?

*The names of all these countries are feminine, but you normally only use **la** with **India**.

Who comes from where?

These are the contestants for an international dancing competition. They have come from all over the world. The compère does not speak any Spanish and does not understand where anyone comes from. Read about the contestants, then see if you can tell him what he wants to know. His questions are beneath the picture.

Angus viene de Escocia.

Estos son Marie y Pierre. Vienen de Francia.

Hari e Indira vienen de la India.

Yuri viene de Hungría. Vive en Budapest.

Franz viene de Austria.

Where do they all come from?

Esta es Lolita. Viene de España.

Where does Franz come from?
What are the Indian contestants called?
Is Lolita Italian or Spanish?

Is there a Scottish contestant?
Where do Marie and Pierre come from?
Who lives in Budapest? Where is Budapest?

Verbs (action words)	singular		hablar	to speak	venir	to come
Spanish verbs change according to who is doing the action. Verbs ending in **ar** follow the same pattern and have the same endings as **hablar**. You will have to learn **venir** by itself.*	I	yo	hablo**	speak	vengo	come
	you	tú	hablas	speak	vienes	come
	you (pol)*	usted	habla	speak	viene	come
	he/she	él/ella	habla	speaks	viene	comes
	plural					
	we (m/f)	nosotros/as	hablamos	speak	venimos	come
	you (m/f)	vosotros/as	habláis	speak	venís	come
	you (pol)*	ustedes	hablan	speak	vienen	come
	they (m/f)	ellos/ellas	hablan	speak	vienen	come

Can you remember?

How would you ask someone where they come from?

Can you say where you come from?
How do you say that you speak Spanish?
How would you ask someone if they can?

*You can find out more about verbs on page 43, and about polite (pol) forms on page 30.
Note that, in Spanish, you often don't need to say "I", "you", "she", etc. So, both **yo hablo and **hablo** mean "I speak".

More about you

Here you can find out how to count up to 20, say how old you are and say how many brothers and sisters you have.

To say how old you are in Spanish, you say how many years you have. So if you are ten, you say **Tengo diez años** (I have ten years).

New words

¿qué edad tienes?	how old are you?
Tengo cinco años	I am five years old
¿tienes..?	have you..?
tengo	I have
no tengo	I have no
el hermano	brother
la hermana	sister
casi	almost
ni	nor
pero	but

Plural words

Most Spanish nouns add an "s" in the plural (when you are talking about more than one person or thing), e.g. **hermano, hermanos**. Those nouns ending in a consonant add "es", e.g. **ciudad, ciudades**. In the plural, the word for "the" is **los** for **el** words and **las** for **la** words.

Numbers**

1	uno/una	11	once
2	dos	12	doce
3	tres	13	trece
4	cuatro	14	catorce
5	cinco	15	quince
6	seis	16	dieciséis
7	siete	17	diecisiete
8	ocho	18	dieciocho
9	nueve	19	diecinueve
10	diez	20	veinte

How old are you?

Have you any brothers and sisters?

*When you ask someone **¿Tienes hermanos?** this means "Have you any brothers or sisters?"
**You will find a complete list of numbers on page 40.

How old are they?

Read what these children are saying, then see if you can say how old they all are.

> Pepe tiene doce años.

> Tenemos quince años.

> Rosa tiene once años.

> Miguel tiene casi catorce años.

> Yo tengo cinco años. Él tiene nueve años.

Miguel   Diana y Silvia   Pepe   Rosa   Luis   Carmen

How many brothers and sisters?

Below you can read how many brothers and sisters the children have. Can you work out who has which brothers and sisters?

Diana y Silvia tienen un hermano y dos hermanas.

Rosa tiene tres hermanas y dos hermanos.

Miguel tiene cinco hermanas, pero no tiene hermanos.

Luis tiene un hermano, pero no tiene hermanas.

Pepe no tiene hermanos ni hermanas, pero tiene un perro.

Useful verbs

tener	to have
yo tengo	I have
tú tienes	you have (singular)
usted tiene	you have (polite)
él/ella tiene	he/she/it has
nosotros/as tenemos	we have
vosotros/as tenéis	you have (plural)
ustedes tienen	you have (pl polite)
ellos/ellas tienen	they have (m/f)

ser*	to be
yo soy	I am
tú eres	you are (singular)
usted es	you are (polite)
él/ella es	he/she/it is
nosotros/as somos	we are
vosotros/as sois	you are (pl plural)
ustedes son	you are (polite)
ellos/ellas son	they are (m/f)

*Ser is used on the next page, so it may help you to learn it now.

Talking about your family

On these two pages you will learn lots of words which will help you to talk about your family. You will also find out how to say "my" and "your" and describe people.

Esta es mi familia.

mi perro

mi abuelo

mi abuela

mi padre

mi madre

mi hermana

mi hermano

mi tío

mi tía

mi gato

Who's who?

¿Es tu hermano?

Sí, es mi hermano.

Y ésta, ¿es tu hermana?

Sí, se llama Natalia.

¿Estos son tus padres?

¡No! Estos son mis abuelos.

New words

la familia	family	**la tía**	aunt	**delgado/a**	thin
el abuelo	grandfather	**los abuelos**	grandparents	**viejo/a**	old
la abuela	grandmother	**los padres**	parents	**joven**	young
el padre	father	**alto/a**	tall	**rubio/a**	blond
la madre	mother	**bajo/a**	short	**moreno/a**	dark-haired
el tío	uncle	**grueso/a**	fat	**cariñoso/a**	friendly

How to say "my" and "your"

The word you use for "my" or "your" depends on whether you are talking about a singular or plural word.

	my	your
singular words	**mi**	**tu**
plural words	**mis**	**tus**

Describing your family

> Mi padre es alto y mi madre es baja.

> Mi madre es alta y mi padre es bajo.

> Mi tío es grueso y mi tía es delgada.

> Mi abuelo es muy viejo. Yo soy joven.

> Mi hermana es rubia. Mi hermano es moreno.

> Mi perro es cariñoso.

Describing words

Most Spanish adjectives change their endings depending on whether they are describing an **el** or **la** word. They end in "**o**" in the masculine form, and this changes to "**a**" in the feminine form.*

Can you describe each of these people in Spanish, starting **Él es …** or **Ella es..**?

*In the word list on page 14, you can see adjectives in the masculine form, followed by the "**a**" for the feminine, e.g. **alto/a**. So the feminine is **alta**. You can find out more about adjectives on pages 42-43.

Your home

Here you can find out how to say what sort of home you live in and where it is. You can also learn what all the rooms are called.

New words

o/u*	or
la casa	house
el apartamento	small flat
el piso	large flat
el castillo	castle
en la ciudad	in the town
en el campo	in the country
a la orilla del mar	by the sea
papá	Dad
mamá	Mum
abuelito	Grandad
abuelita	Granny
el fantasma	ghost
¿dónde estás?	where are you?
el cuarto de baño	bathroom
el comedor	dining room
el dormitorio	bedroom
la sala de estar	living room
la cocina	kitchen
el vestíbulo	hall
arriba	upstairs

Where do you live?

¿Vives en una casa o en un apartamento?

Vivo en una casa.

Vivo en un piso.

Vivo en un castillo.

Town or country?

Vivo en la ciudad.

Vivo en el campo.

Vivo a la orilla del mar.

16   *You only use **u** before words beginning with "**o**" or "**ho**".

Where is everyone?

Papá comes home and wants to know where everyone is. Look at the pictures and see if you can tell him where everyone is, e.g. **La abuelita está en la sala de estar.** Then see if you can answer the questions below the little pictures.

Mamá Papá Abuelito

Abuelita Pedro Isabel

Simón el fantasma

¿Quién está en el comedor?
¿Quién está en la cocina?
¿Quién está en el cuarto de baño?
¿Quién está en el dormitorio?

¿Dónde está la abuelita?
¿Dónde está el fantasma?
¿Dónde está el perro?
¿Dónde está Pedro?
¿Dónde está papá? (Look at the word list)

Can you remember?

How do you ask someone where they live?
How do you ask whether they live in a house or a flat?

Can you remember how to say "in the country"?
Can you remember how to say "in the town"?

How would you tell someone you were upstairs?
How would you tell them you were in the kitchen?

17

Looking for things

Here you can find out how to ask someone what they are looking for and tell them where things are. You can also learn lots of words for things around the house.

New words

buscar	to look for
algo	something
hámster	hamster
encontrar	to find
lo	him/it
sobre	on
debajo de	under
detrás de	behind
delante de	in front of
entre	between
al lado de	next to
la alacena	cupboard
el armario	wardrobe
la butaca	armchair
la cortina	curtain
la planta	plant
el estante	shelf
la mesa	table
la alfombra	carpet
el sofá	sofa
la televisión	television
el teléfono	telephone
el jarrón	vase
¡aquí/allí está!	here/there it is!

¿Él or ella?

There is no special word for "it" in Spanish. You use **él** or **ella** ("he" or "she") depending on whether the word you are replacing is masculine or feminine. You use **él** to replace masculine words and **ella** to replace feminine ones.

¿Esto es para **el** hámster?
Sí, es para **él**.

¿Esto es para **la** tortuga?
Sí, es para **ella**.

The missing hamster

18

In, on or under?

Try to learn these words by heart. **Al lado de** changes to **al lado del** when you put it before an **el** word, e.g. **al lado del sofá** (next to the sofa).

en   *detrás de*   *delante de*   *al lado de*   *debajo de*   *sobre*

Where are they hiding?

Señor López's six pets are hiding somewhere in the room, but he cannot find them. Can you tell him where they are in Spanish, using the words above?

el hámster

el gatito

el perrito

el periquito

la serpiente

la tortuga

el estante

la alacena

la televisión

la alfombra

la butaca

el sofá

el jarrón

el teléfono

la mesa

What do you like eating?

Here you can find out how to say what you like and don't like.

New words

¿le/te gusta?*	do you like?
me gusta	I like
no me gusta**	I don't like
¿qué . . ?	what . . ?
me encanta	I love
en absoluto	not at all
entonces	then
mucho	very much
lo que más	the most
preferir	to prefer
sobre todo	best of all
la ensalada	salad
el pescado	fish
las patatas fritas	chips
el pastel	cake
la salchicha	sausage
el filete	steak
los espaguetis	spaghetti
comer	to eat
la pizza	pizza
la hamburguesa	hamburger
el arroz	rice
el pan	bread
el queso	cheese
yo también	me too

What do you like?

¿Le gusta la ensalada?

¿le gusta el pescado?

No, no me gusta la ensalada.

No, ¡No me gusta en absoluto!

¿Qué le gusta, entonces?

¡Y me encantan los pasteles!

Me gustan las patatas fritas.

What do you like best?

¿Qué le gusta más?

Me gustan mucho las salchichas.

...Pero prefiero el filete.

...Y me gustan sobre todo los espaguetis.

*Among friends, you ask "**¿te gusta..?**" but to be more polite, you would ask "**¿le gusta..?**"
**You can read more about negatives on pages 42-43.

What are they eating?

¿Qué comes?

Como una pizza.

Ella come patatas fritas.

Él come pan y queso.

Nosotros comemos hamburguesas.

Vosotros coméis arroz.

Ellos comen plátanos.

Who likes what?

Who likes cheese? Who doesn't like ham?
Who prefers grapes to bananas?

Can you say in Spanish which things you
like and which you don't like?

A mí también, pero no me gusta el jamón.

Juan

Me gustan los plátanos.

Yo prefiero las uvas.

Me gusta el queso.

Simón

Me gusta sobre todo la tarta de frutas.

Jaime

Abuelito

Isabel

el jamón   la mantequilla   la tarta

el pan   la ensalada   los tomates   el queso

los plátanos   las uvas   una tarta de frutas   el zumo de naranja

Me gusta, me gustan*

Where in English we say "I like", the
Spanish say "(it) pleases me": **me gusta**, or
"(they) please me": **me gustan**.

me gusta/gustan	I like
te gusta/gustan	you like
nos gusta/gustan	we like

*In the same way, to say "I love/like a lot", you say **me encanta** followed by a singular word and **me encantan** followed by a plural.

21

Table talk

Here you can learn all sorts of useful things to say if you are having a meal with Spanish friends or eating out in Spain.

New words

a la mesa, por favor	come to the table, please
tengo hambre	I'm hungry
yo también	me too
sírvete	help yourself
servíos	help yourselves
buen provecho	enjoy your meal
¿me puedes pasar . . .	can you pass me . . .
el agua	water
el pan	bread
el vaso	glass
¿quiere usted* . . . ?	would you like . . . ?
más . . .	some more . . .
la carne	meat
sí, por favor	yes, please
no, gracias	no, thank you
he comido suficiente	I've had enough
¿está bueno?	is it good?
está delicioso	it's delicious

Dinner is ready

Please will you pass me . . .

*Usted is a polite way of saying "you". You can find out more about it on page 30.

Would you like some more?

> ¿Quiere usted más carne?

> Sí, gracias.

> ¿Quiere más patatas fritas?

> No, gracias. He comido suficiente.

> ¿Está bueno?

> Sí, está delicioso.

Who is saying what?

Simón is saying he is hungry.

The chef wants you to enjoy your meal.

Isabel is saying "Help yourself".

Pedro wants someone to pass him a glass.

Mamá is offering Simón more chips.

He says "Yes, please", and that he likes chips.

Then he says "No thanks", he's had enough.

Marcos is saying the food is delicious.

These little pictures show you different things that can happen at mealtime. Practise using the Spanish on these two pages, then cover up your book so you can only see these pictures. Now see if you can say what everyone is saying in Spanish. Remember you can check your answers on page 45.

Your hobbies

These people are talking about their hobbies.

New words

hacer	to do
pintar	to paint
guisar	to cook
la afición	hobby
construir cosas	to make things
bailar	to dance
leer	to read
ver la televisión	to watch TV
tejer	to knit
nadar	to swim
jugar	to play
el deporte	sport
el fútbol	football
el tenis	tennis
la música	music
escuchar	to listen to
el instrumento	instrument
el violín	violin
el piano	piano
por la noche	in the evening
algún(o)/a*	any

hacer (to make or do)

yo hago	I do
tú haces	you do (singular)
usted hace	you do (s polite)
él/ella hace	he/she does
nosotros/as hacemos	we do
vosotros/as hacéis	you do (plural)
ustedes hacen	you do (pl polite)
ellos/ellas hacen	they do

jugar y tocar

When you talk about playing a sport, you say **jugar a** and the name of the sport. **A + el** becomes **al**, e.g. **yo juego al fútbol** (I play football).

To talk about playing an instrument, you say **tocar**, e.g. **yo toco el piano** (I play the piano).

¿Qué te gusta hacer?

Me gusta pintar...

...pero no me gusta guisar.

¿Tienes alguna afición?

Sí, construir cosas...

Y me gusta bailar.

What do you do in the evenings?

¿Qué haces por las noches?

Leo libros...

O veo la televisión y tejo.

*Where in English you ask "Do you have a hobby/play an instrument?", in Spanish you use an extra word: **algún**, and say "Do you have any hobby/play any instrument?"

The sporty type

¿Tienes alguna afición?

Me gusta el deporte.

Yo nado.

Yo juego al fútbol

Y yo juego al tenis.

Music lovers

¿Tienen ustedes aficiones?

Sí, nos gusta escuchar música.

¿Tocan algún instrumento?

Y yo toco el piano.

Sí, yo toco el violín.

What are they doing?

A B C D E

Cover up the rest of the page and see if you can say what all these people are doing in

Spanish, e.g. **Él juega al fútbol.**
What are your hobbies?

Telling the time

Here you can find out how to tell the time in Spanish. You can look up any numbers you don't know on page 40.

There is no word for "past" in Spanish; you just add the number of minutes to the hour: **son las nueve y cinco** (it is five past nine). To say "five to" you say **menos cinco** (less five): **son las nueve menos cinco** (it is five to nine).

New words

¿qué hora es?	what is the time?
es la una	it is one o'clock
son las dos	it is two o'clock
menos cinco	five to
y cuarto	quarter past
menos cuarto	quarter to
y media	half past
mediodía	midday
medianoche	midnight
de la mañana	in the morning
de la noche	in the evening
a	at
levantarse	to get up
su	his/her
desayunar	to have breakfast
almorzar	to have lunch
cenar	to have supper
él va	he goes
al colegio	to school
a la cama	to bed

ir (to go)

yo voy	I go
tú vas	you go (singular)
usted va	you go (s pol)
él/ella va	he/she/it goes
nosotros/as vamos	we go
vosotros/as vais	you go (plural)
ustedes van	you go (pl pol)
ellos/ellas van	they go

What is the time?

Here is how to ask what the time is.

The time is . . .

Son las nueve y cinco.

Son las nueve y cuarto.

Son las nueve y media.

Son las diez menos cuarto.

Son las diez menos cinco.

Es mediodía/ medianoche.

What time of day?

Son las seis de la mañana.

Son las seis de la tarde.

*For one o'clock, midnight and midday, you use the singular verb, e.g. **es la una y diez** (it is ten past one). For other times of day, you use the plural verb, e.g. **son las tres y cuarto** (it is a quarter past three).

Marcos' day

Read what Marcos does throughout the day, then see if you can match each clock with the right picture. You can find out what the answers are on pages 44-45.

a b c d e f g h

1 Marcos se levanta a las siete y media.*

2 Desayuna a las ocho.

3 A las nueve menos cuarto va al colegio.

4 Almuerza** a las doce y media.

5 A las dos y diez juega al fútbol.

6 A las cinco y cuarto ve la televisión.

7 A las seis cena.

8 Se va a la cama a las ocho y media.

What time is it?

Can you say in Spanish what times these clocks show?

a b c g h i k j l d e f m n o

*Some verbs are formed from two parts. You can read about these on pages 42-43.
To learn more about verbs like **almorzar (verbs that sometimes change letters in their stem), see page 43.

Arranging things

Here is how to arrange things with your friends.

New words

¿vamos . . ?	shall we go . . ?
¿cuándo?	when?
el martes	on Tuesday
por la mañana	in the morning
por la tarde	in the afternoon
por la noche	in the evening
la piscina	swimming pool
hacia	at about
hasta el martes	until Tuesday
hoy	today
hasta mañana	until tomorrow
esta tarde	this evening
de acuerdo	O.K.
no puedo	I can't
no es posible	that's no good
¡qué pena!	it's a pity!
ir a	to go to
el cine	cinema
la fiesta	party

Days of the week

domingo	Sunday
lunes	Monday
martes	Tuesday
miércoles	Wednesday
jueves	Thursday
viernes	Friday
sábado	Saturday

Tennis

Swimming

Going to the cinema

28

Going to a party

> ¿Vienes a mi fiesta?

> ¿Cuándo es?

> El sábado por la tarde.

> ¡Qué pena! No es posible.

> El sábado voy a bailar.

Your diary for the week

Here is your diary, showing you what you are doing for a week. Read it, then see if you can answer the questions at the bottom of the page in Spanish.

lunes
16:00 horas. Tenis.

martes
14:00 horas. Piano.
17:30 Piscina.

miércoles
15:00 horas. Tenis.
19:45 Cine.

Jueves

viernes
20:00 Ir a bailar con Jaime.

sabado
14:00 horas. Fútbol.
19:00 horas. Fiesta.

domingo
Tenis por la tarde.

¿Qué haces el viernes?
¿Cuándo juegas al tenis?
¿Cuándo vas al cine?
¿Tocas el piano el jueves?
¿Qué haces el domingo?
¿A qué hora es la fiesta el sábado?

a + el

When **a** comes before **el**, you say **al** instead: **¿vamos al cine?** (shall we go to the cinema?)*

Asking where places are

Here and on the next two pages you can find out how to ask your way around.

New words

perdone	excuse me
de nada	not at all
aquí/allí	here/there
la oficina de correos	post office
en la plaza del mercado	in the market place
el hotel	hotel
después	then
gire . . .	turn . . .
¿hay . . ?	is there . . ?
cerca de aquí	nearby
la calle	street
justo	just
¿está lejos?	is it far?
a cinco minutos	five minutes away
a pie	on foot
el supermercado	supermarket
frente a	opposite
al lado de	next to
el banco	bank
la farmacia	chemist's

How to say "you"

There are four words for "you" in Spanish.* You say **tú** to a friend, but it is more polite to say **usted** to an adult you don't know well. When talking to more than one person you use **vosotros**, or **ustedes** to be more polite.

Directions

todo recto

a la izquierda   **a la derecha**

Being polite

> Perdone, señor . . .

> Gracias.

> De nada.

This is how to say "excuse me". It is best to add **señor**, **señora** or **señorita**.

When people thank you, it is polite to answer **"De nada"**.

Where is . . ?

> Perdone, señora, ¿dónde está la oficina de correos?

> Allí, en la plaza del mercado.

> ¿Dónde está el hotel de la estación, por favor?

> Gire a la izquierda aquí, después siga todo recto.

*See pages 42-43.

Is there a . . . nearby?

Is it far?

Perdone, señor, ¿hay un café cerca de aquí?

¿Está lejos?

Sí, justo a la izquierda en la calle Colón.

No, a cinco minutos a pie.

Perdone, señorita, ¿hay un supermercado cerca de aquí?

Sí, allí, frente al banco.

¿Y una farmacia cerca de aquí?

Justo al lado del supermercado.

Other useful places to ask for

la estación	una gasolinera	los cuartos de baño	un buzón
the station	a petrol station	toilets	a letter box
una cabina telefónica	un camping	el hospital	el aeropuerto
a telephone box	a campsite	the hospital	the airport

Finding your way around

Here you can find out how to ask your way around and follow directions. When you have read everything, try the map puzzle on the opposite page.

*Por favor is the polite way to say "please".

Internet link: watch and listen to a video clip of someone buying a train ticket and learn more about travelling in Spain. Go to **www.usborne-quicklinks.com** for a link to this site.

New words

¿para ir a . . ?	how do I get to . . ?	**hasta**	as far as
tome . . .	take . . .	**en coche**	by car
continúe . . .	carry on . . .	**la primera calle**	the first street
el albergue juvenil	youth hostel	**la segunda calle**	the second street
		la tercera calle	the third street
la oficina de turismo	tourist office	**el Ayuntamiento**	town hall
		la iglesia	church

tomar	to take			When people are telling
				you which way to go, they
yo tomo	I take	**nosotros/as tomamos**	we take	use the command form of
tú tomas	you take (singular)	**vosotros/as tomáis**	you take (plural)	the verb: **Tome ...** (Take ...),
usted toma	you take (s pol)	**ustedes toman**	you take (pl polite)	e.g. **Tome la primera**
él/ella toma	he/she takes	**ellos/ellas toman**	they take (m/f)	**calle ...**

Finding your way around Bahía

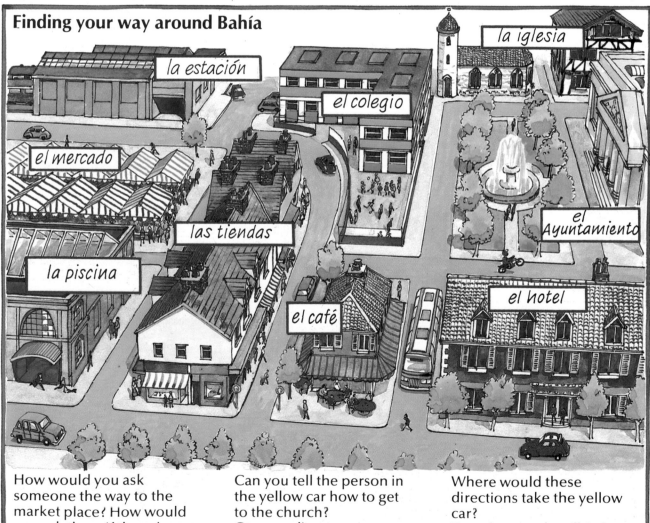

la estación · la iglesia · el colegio · el mercado · el Ayuntamiento · las tiendas · la piscina · el café · el hotel

How would you ask someone the way to the market place? How would you ask them if there is a café nearby? Ask how far it is.

Can you tell the person in the yellow car how to get to the church?
Can you direct someone from the hotel to the market?

Where would these directions take the yellow car?
Tome la segunda calle a la izquierda y está a la derecha.

33

Going shopping

Here and on the next two pages you can find out how to say what you want when you go shopping. When you go into a Spanish shop you should say "**Buenos días, señora**" (or **señor** or **señorita**). If there are lots of people you simply say "**Buenos días**".

Spending money

There are 100 **céntimos** in a **euro**. On price labels, the symbol **€** is used after the price. For example, **dos euros** is written as **2€**, and **dos euros veinte** as **2,20€**. To understand prices you must know the numbers in Spanish. They are listed on page 40.

New words

ir de compras	to go shopping
comprar	to buy
la panadería	baker's
la tienda de comestibles	grocer's
la carnicería	butcher's
la leche	milk
los huevos	eggs
la fruta	fruit
las verduras	vegetables.
la carne	meat
el panecillo	bread roll
la manzana	apple
el tomate	tomato
¿qué desea (usted)?	can I help you?
quiero	I would like
sí, cómo no	with pleasure
¿algo más?	anything else?
¿eso es todo?	is that all?
¿cuánto es?	how much is that?
aquí está/tiene	there you are
un litro	a litre
un kilo	a kilo
medio kilo	half a kilo
entonces	so, well then

Señora Prados goes shopping

La Señora Prados va de compras.

Compra pan en la panadería.

En la panadería

Compra leche y huevos en la tienda de comestibles.

Compra frutas y verduras en el mercado.

Compra carne en la carnicería.

En la tienda de comestibles

¿Qué desea?

Seis huevos, por favor.

¿Algo más, señora?

Un litro de leche, por favor.

¿Cuánto es esto?

Son dos euros veinte.

2.20€

En el mercado

Buenos días, señora. ¿Qué desea?

Un kilo de manzanas, por favor.

¿Algo más, señora?

Medio kilo de tomates.

Entonces, son cuatro euros.

4€

More shopping and going to a café

Here you can find out how to ask how much things cost and how to order things in a café.

New words

costar	to cost
¿cuánto cuesta /cuestan?	how much is /are?
la tarjeta postal	postcard
. . . el kilo	. . . a kilo
. . . cada uno/una	. . . each
la rosa	rose
déme siete	give me seven
el café	coffee
la cuenta	the bill
las uvas	grapes
la naranja	orange
el plátano	banana
la piña	pineapple
el limón	lemon
el melocotón	peach
la limonada	lemonade
la coca-cola	coca-cola
el te	tea
con leche	with milk
con limón	with lemon
el chocolate	hot chocolate
un vaso de	a glass of
un helado	ice cream
aquí lo tiene	here it is

Asking how much things cost

¿Cuánto cuesta* esta tarjeta postal?

Sesenta céntimos.

¿Cuánto cuestan las uvas?

Dos euros treinta el kilo.

2,30€

¿Cuánto cuestan las rosas?

Tres euros diez cada una.

Entonces, déme siete, por favor.

3,10€

Going to a café

¿Qué desea?

Un café, por favor.

¡Aquí lo tiene!

Gracias.

La cuenta, por favor.

Son tres euros.

*To learn more about verbs like **costar** (verbs that sometimes change letters in their stem), see pages 42-43.

Internet link: helpful restaurant words and phrases. Listen to the words spoken, or test yourself with a quiz or a matching game. Go to **www.usborne-quicklinks.com** for a link to this site.

Buying fruit

Everything on the fruit stall is marked with its name and price.

Look at the picture, then see if you can answer the questions below it.

MANZANAS
1,80€ el kilo

¿Qué desea usted?

PLÁTANOS
1,70€ el kilo

UVAS
2,30€ el kilo

NARANJAS
1,90€ el kilo

PIÑAS
2€ cada una

MELO-COTONES
2,10€ el kilo

LIMONES
0,40€
cada uno

How do you tell the stallholder you would like four lemons, a kilo of bananas and a pineapple? How much do each of these things cost?

¿Qué cuesta dos euros cada una?
¿Qué cuesta dos euros diez el kilo?
¿Qué cuesta dos euros treinta el kilo?
¿Qué cuesta cuaranta céntimos?

Things to order

Here are some things you might want to order in a café.

Quiero...

una limonada

una coca-cola

un te con leche

un te con limón

un zumo de naranja

un chocolate

un vaso de leche

un helado

The months and seasons

Here you can learn what the seasons and months are called and find out how to say what the date is.

New words

el mes	month
el año	year
¿cuál es la fecha?	what is the date?
hoy	today
el cumpleaños	birthday

The seasons

la primavera	spring
el verano	summer
el otoño	autumn
el invierno	winter

The months

enero	January
febrero	February
marzo	March
abril	April
mayo	May
junio	June
julio	July
agosto	August
septiembre	September
octubre	October
noviembre	November
diciembre	December

The seasons

la primavera

marzo, abril, mayo . . .

el verano

junio, julio, agosto . . .

el otoño

septiembre, octubre, noviembre . . .

el invierno

diciembre, enero, febrero

First, second, third . . .

primer(o)/a*	first
segundo/a	second
tercer(o)/a*	third
cuarto/a	fourth
quinto/a	fifth
sexto/a	sixth
séptimo/a	seventh
octavo/a	eighth
noveno/a**	ninth
décimo/a	tenth
undécimo/a	eleventh
duodécimo/a	twelfth

To say the date, "the first" is **el primero**, but for all other dates, you just say **el** plus the number.

Enero es el primer mes del año.

Febrero es el segundo mes del año.

Diciembre es el duodécimo mes del año.

Can you say where the rest of the months come in the year?

*When you use **primero** and **tercero** immediately before a masculine singular noun, you shorten them to **primer** and **tercer**.   **There are two words for ninth in Spanish: **noveno/a** and **nono/a**.

What is the date?

> Hoy es el tres de mayo.

> ¿Qué fecha es hoy?

> El primero de enero

Writing the date

Madrid, 4 de mayo

Here you can see how a date is written. You put the number, **de** (of) and the month.

When is your birthday?

> ¿Cuándo es tu cumpleaños?

> Es el diez de noviembre.

> Mi cumpleaños es el doce de febrero.

> El cumpleaños de Simón es el ocho de junio.

When are their birthdays?

The dates of the children's birthdays are written below their pictures. Can you say in Spanish when they are, e.g. **El cumpleaños de Marisa es el dos de abril.**

Marisa	Armando	Elena	Clara	Carlos	Roberto
el 2 de abril	el 21 de junio	el 18 de octubre	el 31 de agosto	el 3 de marzo	el 7 de septiembre

Colours and numbers

Internet link: test your numbers from 0 to 100 and match the pairs in a word game. Go to **www.usborne-quicklinks.com** for a link to this site.

Colours are describing words, so they end in "o" when they refer to an **el** word and in "a" when they refer to a **la** word. If a colour ends in "e", "a" or in a consonant, the ending doesn't change.

The colours

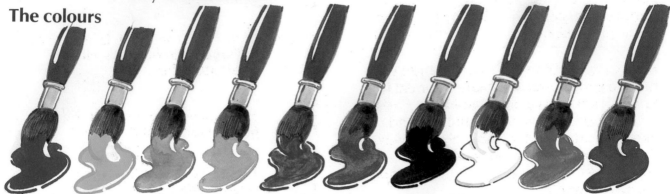

rojo(a)   azul   amarillo(a)   verde   naranja   rosa   negro(a)   blanco(a)   gris   marrón

What colour is it?

Cover the picture above and see if you can say what colour everything is in the painting. You should know all the words you need.*

Numbers

You count the 30s, 40s etc. to the 90s in the same way as 30 to 39: **treinta y uno** (31), **treinta y dos** (32), **treinta y tres** (33), etc.

1 uno	11 once	21 veintiuno	41 cuarenta y uno
2 dos	12 doce	22 veintidós	50 cincuenta
3 tres	13 trece	23 veintitrés	51 cincuenta y uno
4 cuatro	14 catorce	24 veinticuatro	60 sesenta
5 cinco	15 quince	25 veinticinco	70 setenta
6 seis	16 dieciséis	26 veintiséis	80 ochenta
7 siete	17 diecisiete	27 veintisiete	90 noventa
8 ocho	18 dieciocho	28 veintiocho	100 cien
9 nueve	19 diecinueve	29 veintinueve	200 doscientos
10 diez	20 veinte	30 treinta	300 trescientos
		31 treinta y uno	400 cuatrocientos
		40 cuarenta	500 quinientos

*The sky is **el cielo**.

Pronunciation guide

In Spanish many letters are pronounced differently. The best way to learn to speak Spanish is to listen carefully to Spanish people and copy what they say, but here are some general points to help you.

Below is a list of letters with a guide to how to pronounce each one. For each Spanish sound we have shown an English word, or part of a word, which sounds like it. Read it out loud in a normal way to find out how to pronounce the Spanish sound, then practise saying the examples shown beneath.

á   A mark like this above a vowel is called a stress mark. It means you should stress this part of the word.

a   Like the "a" sound in "hat": **gracias, casa, vaso**

e   Like the "a" sound in "care": **señor, tener, tres**

i   Like the "ee" sound in "feet": **tía, oficina, amarillo**

o   Like the "o" in "got": **moreno, limón, mayo**

u   Like the "oo" in "moon": **una, lunes, uvas**

ce, ci   Before "i" or "e", "c" is like the "th" in thumb: **alacena, cine**

ca, co, cu   Before other letters it is like the "c" in "cat": **toca, coche, cuenta**

ga, go, gu   Before "a", "o" or "u", "g" sounds like the "g" in "ghost": **gato, agosto, agua**

ge, gi   Before "e" or "i", "g" sounds like the "ch" in "loch": **gente, girar**

gue, gui   Before "ue" or "ui", it is like the "g" in "great" and the "u" is silent: **albergue, guisar**

h   This is never pronounced: so **hombre** sounds like "ombre".

j   This is like the "ch" in "loch": **pájaro, verja, tejer**

ll   Like the "y" in "yes": **lleno, llamar, calle**

ñ   Like the "ni" sound in "onion": **señor, baño, piña**

qu   Like the "k" in "kit", and the "u" is silent: **mantequilla, izquierda, qué**

r, rr   A trilling sound made by putting your tongue behind your upper teeth: **río, marzo, perro**

v/b   "B" and "v" both sound like the "b" in big: **vaso, bailar**

y   When it is alone or at the end of a word "y" is a vowel and it sounds like the "ee" in "feet": **y**

When it comes in the middle of a word, it sounds like the "y" in "yesterday": **mayo**

z   Like the "th" sound in "thunder": **buzón, zumo**

Grammar

Internet links: *more helpful hints on grammar and verb conjugation. Go to* **www.usborne-quicklinks.com** *for links to these sites.*

Grammar is like a set of rules about how you put words together and it is different for every language. You will find Spanish easier if you learn some of its grammar, but don't worry if you don't understand all of it straightaway. Just read a little about it at a time. This is a summary of the grammar used in this book.

el, la

In Spanish nouns are either masculine (m) or feminine (f). Most nouns ending in **o** are masculine, and those ending in **a**, **d** or **ción** are usually feminine.* With other endings you have to learn whether the noun is (m) or (f) as you go. It is best to learn the word for "the" with each noun. "The" is **el** before (m) nouns and **la** before (f) nouns.

el libro	the book
la camisa	the shirt

los, las

When talking about more than one thing, the word for "the" is **los** for (m) words and **las** for (f) words.

los libros	the books
las camisas	the shirts

To make a noun plural, you add **s** to words ending in a vowel, and **es** to words ending in a consonant.

la casa	**las casas**
la ciudad	**las ciudades**

un, una

The Spanish for "a" or "an" is **un** before (m) nouns and **una** before (f) nouns.

un libro	a book
una camisa	a shirt

al, del

If **el** comes after **a** (to, at), it becomes **al**:

Juan va al supermercado	John goes to the supermarket.

If **el** comes after **de** (of, from), it becomes **del**:

debajo del sofá	under the sofa

Pronouns

Here are pronouns you should know:

singular						plural				
yo	I	**tú**	you (for a friend)	**él**	he, it (m)	**nosotros/as**	we			
		usted	you (polite)	**ella**	she, it (f)	**vosotros/as**	you (for friends)	**ellos**	they (m)	
						ustedes	you (polite)	**ellas**	they (f)	

You can find out more about **él** and **ella** for "it" on page 18. Saying "you" to friends and to people you don't know well (when you use the polite form) is explained on page 30. How you choose between **ellos** and **ellas** ("they" masculine and "they" feminine) is explained on page 6.

Adjectives

An adjective is a describing word. Spanish adjectives change their endings depending on whether they are describing an (m) or (f) word and whether the word is singular (s) or plural (pl). In word lists, the masculine singular adjective is shown. These usually end in **o**. To make an adjective feminine, you normally drop the **o** and add an **a**. To make these adjectives plural, you add an **s**.

el niño contento	the happy boy
la niña contenta	the happy girl
los niños contentos	the happy children

If an adjective ends in **e**, it only changes in the plural. To make these adjectives plural, you add an **s**.

el libro grande	the big book
la casa grande	the big house
las casas grandes	the big houses

Adjectives ending in a consonant also only change in the plural. These take **es**:

el brazo débil	the weak arm
la gata débil	the weak cat
los animales débiles	the weak animals

*But **la mano** (hand) is feminine, and **el día** (day), is masculine.

My, your

The word for "my" or "your" depends on whether the word that follows it is singular or plural:

mi/tu hermana	my/your sister
mis/tus abuelos	my/your grandparents

Verbs

Spanish verbs (doing words) change according to who is doing the action. Most of them follow regular patterns and have the same endings. The main type of verb used in this book ends in **ar**, like **hablar** (to speak). You can see what the different endings are here.

There are some verbs in this book that do not follow this pattern. It is best to learn these as you go along.

hablar	to speak
yo hablo	I speak
tú hablas	you speak (singular)
usted habla	you speak (s polite)
él/ella habla	he/she/it/speaks
nosotros/as hablamos	we speak
vosotros/as habláis	you speak (plural)
ustedes hablan	you speak (pl polite)
ellos/ellas hablan	they speak (m/f)

Negative verbs

To make a verb negative in Spanish, e.g. to say "I do not ...", "he does not ...", you put **no** immediately before the verb:

Yo no hablo español	I do not speak Spanish.
No están contentos.	They are not happy.

Stem-changing verbs

Some verbs change their stem (the part remaining after the **ar** is dropped). In verbs with an **e** in the stem, the **e** changes to **ie**. In verbs with an **o** in the stem, the **o** changes to **ue**. The **nosotros** and **vosotros** forms of the verb don't change.

pensar (ie)   to think
pienso, piensas, piensa, pensamos, pensáis, piensan

contar (ue)   to count
cuento, cuentas, cuenta, contamos, contáis, cuentan

Reflexive verbs

These are verbs that always have a special pronoun in front of them. Where in English we say "I sit down", the Spanish say "I sit myself down": **me siento**. The pronoun changes according to who is doing the action but **me** always goes with **yo** and **te** with **tú** etc., as you can see on the right.

You will notice these verbs in the Glossary of this book because of the **se** that appears at the end of them.

sentar(se)	to sit down
(yo) me siento	I sit down
(tú) te sientas	you sit down (singular)
(usted) se sienta	you sit down (s polite)
(él/ella) se sienta	he/she/it sits down
(nosotros/as) nos sentamos	we sit down
(vosotros/as) os sentáis	you sit down (plural)
(ustedes) se sientan	you sit down (pl polite)
(ellos/ellas) se sientan	they sit down

Estar and ser

There are two verbs meaning "to be" in Spanish: **ser** and **estar**.

Ser is used to describe people and things and for telling the time.

Estar is used to say where people and things are (e.g. "He is in America") and to describe something which will not last long, (e.g. "It is raining").

estar	ser	to be
estoy*	**soy**	I am
estás	**eres**	you are (singular)
está	**es**	you are (polite)
está	**es**	he/she/it is
estamos	**somos**	we are
estáis	**sois**	you are (plural)
están	**son**	you are (pl polite)
están	**son**	they are (m/f)

*Remember that in Spanish, you don't always say "I", "you", "he" etc. ... before the verb. The verb alone can make this clear.

Answers to puzzles

p.7

What are they called?

Él se llama Pedro.
Ella se llama María.
Ellos se llaman Pablo y Juan.
Yo me llamo (your name).

Who is who?

Miguel is talking to Juan.
Ana is talking to Amalia.
Miguel is next to the seal.
Juan is talking to him.
Ana is at the bottom left-hand corner.
The man talking to Nicolás is going home.

Can you remember?

¿Cómo te llamas?
Yo me llamo . . .
Es mi amiga. Se llama Amalia.
Mi amigo se llama Daniel.

p.9

Can you remember?

la/una flor, el/un gato, el/un árbol, el/un nido,
el/un pájaro, el/un tejado, el Sol, la/una
ventana, el/un coche, el/un perro.

p.11

Who comes from where?

Franz comes from Austria.
They are called Hari and Indira.
Lolita is Spanish.
Yes, Angus comes from Scotland.
Marie and Pierre come from France.
Yuri lives in Budapest.
Budapest is in Hungary.

Can you remember?

¿De dónde eres?
Soy de . . .
Hablo español.
¿Hablas español?

p.13

How old are they?

Miguel is 13. Diana and Silvia are 15. Pepe is
12. Rosa is 11. Luis is 9. Carmen is 5.

How many brothers and sisters?

A = Diana y Silvia. B = Luis. C = Miguel.
D = Pepe. E = Rosa.

p.17

Where is everyone?

Simón está en la cocina.
El abuelito está en el comedor.
Mamá está en el dormitorio.
La abuelita está en la sala de estar.
El fantasma está en el dormitorio de Isabel.
Isabel está arriba.
Pedro está en el cuarto de baño.

Abuelito. Simón. Pedro. Mamá.

En la sala de estar.
En el dormitorio de Isabel.
En el comedor.
En el cuarto de baño.
En el vestíbulo.

Can you remember?

¿Dónde vives?
¿Vives en una casa o en un apartamento?
En el campo.
En la ciudad.
Yo estoy arriba.
Yo estoy en la cocina.

p.19

Where are they hiding?

El hámster está en el jarrón.
El gatito está detrás de la televisión.
El perrito está en la alacena.
El periquito está sobre el estante.
La serpiente está detrás del sofá.
La tortuga está al lado del teléfono.

p.21

Who likes what?

1.Jaime. 2.Juan. 3.Abuelito.

p.23

Who is saying what?

"Tengo hambre."
"Buen provecho."
"Sírvete."
"¿Me puedes pasar un vaso?"
"¿Quieres más patatas fritas?"
"Sí, gracias. Me gustan las patatas fritas."
"No, gracias. He comido suficiente."
"Está delicioso."

p.25

What are they doing?

A Él guisa. B Él nada. C Ellos bailan.
D Ella toca el violín. E Él pinta.

p.27

Marco's day

1b, 2e, 3f, 4a, 5h, 6g, 7d, 8c.

What time is it?
A Son las tres y cinco.
B Son las once y cinco.
C Son las nueve menos diez.
D Son las cuatro menos cuarto.
E Son las tres y veinticinco.
F Son las siete y media.
G Son las tres.
H Son las cuatro.
I Son las nueve.
J Es la una y media.
K Son las siete y cinco.
L Son las diez y media.
M Son las seis.
N Son las cuatro menos veinticinco.
O Son las dos menos cinco.

p.29

El viernes por la tarde voy a bailar con Jaime.
Juego al tenis el lunes, el miércoles y el
domingo.

Voy al cine el miércoles por la tarde.
No, toco el piano el martes.
El domingo por la tarde juego al tenis.
Es a las siete.

p.33

¿Cómo se va a la plaza del mercado, por favor?
Perdone, ¿hay un café cerca de aquí?
¿Está lejos?
Tome la tercera calle a la izquierda, después
siga todo recto.
Tome la tercera calle a la derecha, después siga
todo recto. El mercado está a la izquierda.
To the school.

p.37

Quiero cuatro limones, un kilo de plátanos y
una piña.
Cuatro limones cuestan un euro sesenta.
Un kilo de plátanos cuesta un euro setenta.
Una piña cuesta dos euros.

una piña. los melocotones. las uvas. un limón.

p.39

El cumpleaños de Marisa es el dos de abril.
El cumpleaños de Armando es el veintiuno de
junio.
El cumpleaños de Elena es el dieciocho de
octubre.
El cumpleaños de Clara es la treinta y uno de
agosto.
El cumpleaños de Carlos es el tres de marzo.
El cumpleaños de Roberto es el siete de
septiembre.

p.40

La calle es gris.
El Sol es amarillo.
El tejado es naranja.
El cielo es azul.
Las flores son rosas.
El perro es marrón.
El pájaro es negro.
El coche es rojo.
Los árboles son verdes.
La casa es blanca.

Glossary

Adjectives are shown in their masculine singular form. In general, you change the masculine ending **o** to **a** to make them feminine.

a	at, to
a la derecha	on the right
a la izquierda	on the left
a la orilla del mar	by the sea
a pie	on foot
abril	April
la abuela	grandmother
la abuelita	Granny
el abuelito	Grandad
el abuelo	grandfather
los abuelos	grandparents
la afición	hobby
agosto	August
el agua	water
al lado de	next to
la alacena	cupboard
el albergue juvenil	youth hostel
alemán	German
Alemania	Germany
la alfombra	carpet
¿ algo más ?	anything else ?
algún	any
alguna cosa or algo	something
allí	over there
el almuerzo	lunch
alto	tall
amarillo	yellow
el amigo, la amiga	friend (m/f)
el año	year
el apartamento	flat
aproximadamente	about
aquí	here
el árbol	tree
el armario	wardrobe
arriba	upstairs
el arroz	rice
Austria	Austria
azul	blue
bailar	to dance
el banco	bank
bien	good, well
blanco	white
¡Buen provecho!	Enjoy your meal!
buenas noches	good evening, good night
buenas tardes	good afternoon
buenos días	hello, good morning
buscar	to look for
la butaca	armchair
el buzón	post box
la cabina telefónica	telephone box
cada uno	each (one)
el café	café, coffee

la calle	street
la cama	bed
el camping	campsite
cariñoso	friendly
la carne	meat
la carnicería	butcher's
la casa	house
casi	almost
el castillo	castle
la cena	supper, dinner
cerca de aquí	nearby
la chimenea	chimney
el chocolate	chocolate
el cielo	sky
el cine	cinema
la coca-cola	coca-cola
el coche	car
la cocina	kitchen
cocinar	to cook
el colegio	school
el comedor	dining room
comer	to eat
¿cómo estás?	how are you?
¿cómo te llamas?	what is your name?
comprar	to buy
con	with
construir cosas	to make things
la cortina	curtain
costar(ue)	to cost
¿cuándo?	when?
¿cuánto?	how much?
el cuarto de baño	bathroom
la cuenta	bill
el cumpleaños	birthday
de acuerdo	O.K.
de nada	not at all (in answer to "gracias")
¿de dónde?	from where?
debajo de	under
delante de	in front of
delgado	thin
el deporte	sport
el desayuno	breakfast
después	then
detrás de	behind
diciembre	December
el domingo	Sunday
¿dónde?	where?
el dormitorio	bedroom
el	the (masculine)
en	in
en el campo	in the country
en español	in Spanish
en la ciudad	in the town
encantar	to love, like a lot
encontrar(ue)	to find
enero	January
la ensalada	salad
entonces	then
entre	between